My
Flute

Sri Chinmoy

My Flute

Sri Chinmoy

Cover photo: Shraddha

ISBN 0-88497-227-5

Published by:
Aum Publications

CONTENTS

INTRODUCTION

My eternal days are found in speeding time,
I play upon His Flute of rhapsody.

Here is a great Yogi: like us, a man whose physical existence is finite, but unlike us, whose consciousness, liberated and divinised, represents the Infinite. Sri Chinmoy is not only a God-realised Master, but to those who understand him deeply and soulfully, he is the chosen representative of the Supreme. He has been chosen to offer to humanity a spiritual consciousness never before brought down to earth.

Spiritual Masters are not expected to be writers, poets or musicians, and most of them are not. Rarely does it happen that a person of such great spiritual heights is also endowed with literary and musical gifts. Sri Chinmoy is one of the few exceptions. His extraordinary literary capacity in the spiritual field has already been widely recognised by true seekers of the Supreme, and his growing influence as a composer and singer of soul-elevating songs is inspiring great numbers of music-loving aspirants.

But here in this book of poetry, we see another facet of Sri Chinmoy's rare spiritual personality. Through the poet's direct intensity and sweetness, he expresses the highest sublimities of divine realisation; through the meters and cadences of poetic form, he brings us the music of the Beyond. Such capacity is granted only to the exceptional soul. Sri Chinmoy clothes with living imagery the most exalted states of existence.

Drunk deep of Immortality,
I am the root and boughs of a teeming vast.

In him is the mingling of the purest fountain-sources, human and divine: he captures the Beyond and makes it accessible to our human understanding; he gives form to the formless.

At will I break and build my symbol sheath
And freely enjoy the world's unshadowed fun.

The Truth immutable is revealed;
I am the Way, the God-Soul.

I face the One alone.

What is most significant is that he uses the simplest human words, the humblest poetic forms, to embody and convey a state of consciousness far above and beyond the human.

My spirit aware of all the heights,
I am mute in the core of the Sun.

I barter nothing with time and deeds;
    My cosmic play is done.

This is the miracle of this *Kavi* (seer-poet) of the twentieth century, who has not only seen the Beyond but has grown into the Beyond.

In this book of poetry perhaps the most significant achievement, and certainly the one which will prove of deepest value to the aspirant, is the voicing of Sri Chinmoy's compassionate identification with the wavering pilgrim on the spiritual path. All the doubts, fears, limitations and darknesses which are experienced by every disciple on the path are caught by the Master's loving embrace.

A raft am I on the sea of Time,
My oars are washed away.

.·—―·.

Another day, another day,
My Lord Supreme is far away.

.·—―·.

A little joy have I of ceaseless joy,
    A little day of timeless day.
Yet knows no bounds this empty show of mine;
    I march along a goalless way.

In becoming one with our weaknesses, he shows us how to transcend them. In fact, he transcends them for us. His students know and feel that Sri Chinmoy does this very thing in their daily lives of multifarious activities. In his poems and in his divine mission on earth, he identifies himself with suffering and aspiring humanity, and in so doing, he offers us the key to open the Door of the Absolute. He carries us to the Abode of the sole Reality. His heart is of us. His life is for us. He transmutes our suffering into divine Delight.

In Sri Chinmoy the seer-poet, and in Sri Chinmoy the spiritual liberator, we find the meeting place of earth's throbbing pangs and Heaven's assuring Smile.

Alo Devi Siddha
1972

My
Flute

Sri Chinmoy

THE ABSOLUTE

No mind, no form, I only exist;
  Now ceased all will and thought.
The final end of Nature's dance,
  I am It whom I have sought.

A realm of Bliss bare, ultimate,
  Beyond both knower and known.
A rest immense I enjoy at last;
  I face the One alone.

I have crossed the secret ways of life,
  I have become the Goal.
The Truth immutable is revealed;
  I am the way, the God-Soul.

My spirit aware of all the heights,
  I am mute in the core of the Sun.
I barter nothing with time and deeds;
  My cosmic play is done.

SWEET, SWEETER, SWEETEST

Sweet is my Lord.
Him I have realised as the Eternal Truth.

Sweeter is my Lord.
Him I have realised as the only Doer.

Sweetest is my Lord.
Him I have realised as the Enjoyer Supreme.

MY NAME, MY AGE, MY HOME

At last I know my name.
My name is God's eternal Game.
At last I know my name.

At last I know my age.
My age is Infinity's page.
At last I know my age.

At last I know my home.
My home is where my flame-worlds roam.
At last I know my home.

O LOVE ME MORE AND LOVE ME LONG

O love me more and love me long.
My boat is sinking, my hope is strong.

O love me more and love me long.
My breath is bleeding, my dream is strong.

O love me more and love me long.
My soul is leaving, my surrender strong.

O love me more and love me long.
My Goal is crying, my promise strong.

ANOTHER DAY

Another day, another day,
My Lord Supreme is far away.

Another day, my heart can be
The all-giving breath of patience-tree.

Another day, my life can feed
My soulful world with its crying need.

Another day, I pine to hear
God's Voice of Light and feel Him near.

Another day, another day,
My tears shall win His blue-gold Ray.

Another day, another day,
And then, no more my ignorance-clay.

Another day, I'll be God's Love
Within, without, below, above.

APOCALYPSE

Within, without the cosmos wide am I;
In joyful sweep I loose forth and draw back all.
A birthless, deathless Spirit that moves and is still
Ever abides within to hear my call.

I who create on earth my joys and doles
To fulfil my matchless quest in all my play,
I veil my face of truth with golden hues
And see the serpent-night and python-day.

A Consciousness-Bliss I feel in each breath;
I am the self-amorous child of the Sun.
At will I break and build my symbol sheath
And freely enjoy the world's unshadowed fun.

I AM A THIEF

I am a thief; I steal every night.
Each theft of mine kindles a thrill
On the Supreme's all-fulfilling Eye.
What do I steal? His Grace, my meal.

Why do I steal? He compels me so.
Perhaps He finds no other way
To feed my Spirit's hunger stark
With the Nectar of His shadowless Ray.

I AM A FOOL

I am a fool, they say.
Am I, am I a fool?
I go to my inner School;
God's Eye my eternal Day.

To help my Lord in His Play,
To found His Smile on earth,
My divinely human birth.
Yet I am a fool, they say.

I AM AN IDIOT

I know I am an idiot true.
In the growing clouds my hopeful feet,
Hands flung skywards for the blue stars.
My throes no sun, no moon, shall greet.

I had a dream, a real dream:
God would bury Himself to live
In human ignorance hungry and black,
To human death His Soul He'd give.

IMMORTALITY

I feel in all my limbs His boundless Grace;
Within my heart the Truth of life shines white.
The secret heights of God my soul now climbs;
No dole, no sombre pang, no death in my sight.

No mortal days and nights can shake my calm;
A Light above sustains my secret soul.
All doubts with grief are banished from my deeps.
My eyes of light perceive my cherished Goal.

Though in the world, I am above its woe;
I dwell in an ocean of supreme release.
My mind, a core of the One's unmeasured Thoughts;
The star-vast welkin hugs my Spirit's peace.

My eternal days are found in speeding time;
I play upon His Flute of rhapsody.
Impossible deeds no more impossible seem;
In birth-chains now shines Immortality.

A LITTLE

A little joy have I of ceaseless joy,
   A little day of timeless day.
Yet knows no bounds this empty show of mine;
   I march along a goalless way.

O Love! A desert within me ever pines.
   Do turn it into a song of dawn.
I know not in what hour of evil night
   Thou art, my Lord, from me withdrawn.

Life now must reach Thy Breath of Bliss supreme,
   Make Thee the one and only Guide.
Thou art the Bridge between my death and birth.
   O let my longings in Thee abide.

STRUGGLE'S GLOOM

With a blank sorrow, heavy I am now grown;
Like things eternal, changeless stands my woe.
In vain I try to overcome my foe.
O Lord of Love! Make me more dead than stone.

Thy Grace of silent Smile I never feel;
The forger of evil stamps my nights and days.
His call my sleepless body ever obeys.
My heart I annihilate and try to heal.

The dumb earth-waste now burns a hell to my soul.
I fail to fight with its stupendous doom,
My breath is a slave of that unending gloom.
For Light I pine, but find a tenebrous goal.

Smoke-clouds cover my face of Spirit's fire;
Naked I move in night's ignorance deep and dire.

THE SUPREME

Father, I have seen.
"No."
Father, I have known.
"No."
Father, I have felt.
"No."
Father, I have become.
"No."
Father, I Am.
"Yes."

THE SUPREME

Father, You are the Grace.
"No."
Father, You are the Law.
"No."
Father, You are the Birth
and
Death of Creation.
"No."
Father, You are the Child
of
Your DREAM.
"Yes."

BETWEEN NOTHINGNESS
AND ETERNITY

Barren of events,
Rich in pretensions
My earthly life.

Obscurity
My real name.

Wholly unto myself
I exist.

I wrap no soul
In my embrace.

No mentor worthy
Of my calibre
Have I.

I am all alone
Between failure
And frustration.

I am the red thread
Between Nothingness
And Eternity.

THE WORLD-LORD

O my body,
You are the home of the river of tears.

O my vital,
You are the song of the heartless city.

O my mind,
You are the forest of tenebrous night.

O my heart,
You are the love of the World-Lord.

REVEALING SOUL
AND
FULFILLING GOAL

If You but knew, Father,
What I have done for You:
Planted and raised a climbing tree
For You to dance on its top, smiling free.

If You but knew, Father,
What I have done for You.
I have become the world's lowest slave,
Your Breath to serve in man, the grave.

"If you but knew, child,
What I ever think of you.
You are My Life's revealing Soul,
You are My Vision's fulfilling Goal."

EVER AND NEVER

Will You love me, Lord,
If I love ignorance more?
  "I shall love you,
To you open My Spirit's Door."

Will You love me, Lord,
If I marry the fires of hell?
  "I shall love you;
Your life's venom-tree My Eye shall fell."

Will You love me, Lord,
If I live with wildest death?
  "I shall love you;
In you I sowed My deathless Breath."

Will You love me, Lord,
If I come to You alone?
  "Never! Bring quick
With you the world, else I shall moan."

NEVER TO MEET AGAIN

Never to meet again:
My yesterday's face,
My backward race,
Never to meet again.

Never to meet again:
Swift fear the thief,
Wild doubt the chief,
Never to meet again.

Never to meet again:
The clasp of death
And Satan's breath,
Never to meet again.

Never to meet again:
Chinmoy the failure,
Ignorance pure,
Never to meet again.

BEFORE THE END OF DAY

Before the end of day
My eye of Light shall change
My face of sombre clay
And touch my Spirit's range.

BEFORE THE END OF NIGHT

Before the end of night
I can, I shall devour
Sleepless death, senseless bite;
In me my Supreme, my Power.

TRANSFORMATION-LIGHT

O blind and dark night of our heart's abyss!
We are the comrades of the river of tears.
In the clime of binding attachment,
Crying and smiling we kindle the lamp
    Of wild obstruction-shades.
Our world is an empty hope, destitute.
We shall be the language-message
    Of the Time Eternal.
We shall grow into infinite Hunger,
    Infinite Nectar-Delight
And Eternity's Transformation-Light.

THE HERO MARCHES ALONG

He who has loved this world
Has only got excruciating pangs.
The world has thrown on him
All ugliness, filth, dirt and impurity.
Yet the hero marches along,
Carrying the burden of the entire world.
At the end of his teeming struggles
He will go and stand at the Feet
  Of the Lord Supreme.

THE MOTHER SUPREME

Soul-stirring eyes of gold Delight,
All-where reigning supreme—
Our blind secrecy's dream
She seizes with Her all-forgiving Sight.

Torn now asunder our ego's screen,
Under Her Smile of Grace
Blooms quick our surrender's face.
She paves the way to a life evergreen.

O LIGHT OF THE SUPREME!

O Beauty *non-pareil*, O Beloved,
Do burn the fire of beauty and splendour
  Within my heart.
By loving You, eternally beautiful I shall be.
May Lord Shiva's destruction-dance
Destroy all shackles of the finite.
May the Light of the Supreme inundate me,
My heart, my heart, my all.
Having loved the Infinite,
The heart of gloom is crying
  For the bloom of Light.
O Life Infinite, give me the eternal hunger,
  Aspiration-cry.
The tiniest drop will lose its *raison d'être*
In the heart of the boundless ocean.
In fire and air Your Life of the Spirit I behold.
O Beauty, O Beauty's Gold,
O Light of the Supreme!

HOPE

Thou art my Lord, my golden dream,
   Thou art my life in death.
O bless me with Thy Hope supreme,
   Lord of the Eternal Breath!

Agelong the vision of Thy Sun
   For darkness have I sought.
I know the evils I should shun
   And quickly bring to nought.

The earth is deaf and blind, my Lord;
   Its true goal it denies.
It hears no voice, no Heavenly word
   From those who seek the skies.

O yet I feel Thy kingly Grace
   With my feeble mortality.
I shall win at last the noonward race,
   Plunge in the Nectar-Sea.

NEVER THE SAME AGAIN

Never the same again,
Lost peace restored.
Never the same again.

Never the same again,
Lost joy regained.
Never the same again.

Never the same again,
Lost power reborn.
Never the same again.

EVER THE SAME AGAIN

Ever the same again,
My lost Truth rediscovered.
Ever the same again.

Ever the same again,
My forgotten Self remembered.
Ever the same again.

Ever the same again,
My lost Goal regained.
Ever the same again.

O BIRD OF LIGHT

One thought, one tune, one resonance—
Who calls me ever and anon?
I know not where I am.
I know not whither I shall go.
In dark amnesia,
Myself I buy, myself I sell.
All I break, again all I build.
All I hope to be mine, mine alone.
Alas, my heart is eclipsed
By dark and wild destruction-night.

O Bird of Light, O Bird of Light,
With your glowing and flowing flames
Do enter into my heart once again.
You are calling me to climb up
And fly into the blue.
But how can I?
My heart is in prison,
In the strangled breath of a tiny room.
O Bird of Light, O Bird of Light,
O Bird of Light Supreme,
In me, I pray, keep not an iota of gloom.

ARISE! AWAKE!

Arise, awake, O friend of my dream.
Arise, awake, O breath of my life.
Arise, awake, O light of my eyes.
O seer-poet in me,
Do manifest yourself in me and through me.

Arise, awake, O vast heart within me.
Arise, awake, O consciousness of mine,
Which is always transcending the universe
And its own life of the Beyond.

Arise, awake, O form of my meditation
    transcendental.
Arise, awake, O bound divinity in humanity.
Arise, awake, O my heart's Liberator, Shiva,
And free mankind from its ignorance-sleep.

AN OPEN INVITATION

Each soul, a striking page
In perfection-book of Fate.
Each prayer, a tender knock
At God's own psychic Gate.

Each thought dauntless shall live
In Truth, ignorant of fall.
God comes Himself to receive;
The Promised Land is for all.

FEAR

Whom do I fear?
The Lord, the One?
Not true! I am
My Father's son.

What do I fear?
My ignorance vast—
The sleepless spear,
The eyeless dust.

Why do I fear?
Because my eyes
See not the smile
Of the golden skies.

And what is fear?
A tempting call
From the bondage-sphere
Of an airtight ball.

And where is fear?
It is everywhere,
Death's atmosphere,
Shameless and bare.

FOUR EYES

God's Tears
In doubting eyes.

God's Hope
In aspiring eyes.

God's Smile
In conquering eyes.

But God
In all-giving eyes.

GOD'S ABSENCE AND GOD'S PRESENCE

O Lord, Thy absence has measureless power.
Pangs of bitter failures rage through my mind.
Hot knives stab through my heart with every breath.
I know, I know, I am the eternal blind.

O Lord, Thy Presence has fathomless power.
Who says my soul is limp with black despair?
Eternity sits at my feet like a slave,
And Death, a weeping child—helpless, bare.

IN THE FOREST OF MY INNER LIGHT

O King of the cowherds,
O King of the cowherds,
Just once before me appear.
My life is a false dream,
My death is a false dream.
Do take them away.

O King of the cowherds,
O King of the cowherds,
Just once before me appear.
In the forest of my inner light,
In the silent depths of my heart,
I hear the soul-stirring music of Your Flute.

I see Your divine Cow,
Grazing in the lap of Infinity's Silence.
O King of the cowherds,
O King of the cowherds,
Just once before me appear.

I CAME

Into the world of beauty's flame,
Into the world of offering's game,
Into the world of lustre-flood
I came, I came, my existence came.

I LOST

I lost my soul when I was born.
I lost my heart when earth I embraced.
I lost my Goal when doubt I fed.
I lost my All when hope I chased.

LEAVE ME ALONE

Leave me alone, leave me alone.
I need my rest in my soaring nest.
My bleeding heart for God's bending Ears.
His Heart my host, His Soul my guest.

Leave me alone, my play is done.
O world, no more shall I stab your pride.
Your lessons wild are harrows of death
I shall unlearn—in God to hide.

Leave me alone, leave me alone.
I have now seen my soul's highest Goal.
In the glow and flow of Silence-Sea
My life of cries has found its role.

MY KRISHNA IS NOT BLACK

My Krishna is not black,
He is pure gold.
He Himself is woven
Into the universal Beauty, Light and Splendour.

He looks dark
Because I have spilled the ink
Of my mind on Him.
Otherwise, my Beloved is All-Light.

He created light and darkness,
He is within and without the Cosmos vast.

With this knowledge,
I will have a new acquaintance
With the world at large.

MY LIFE

My life began with duty's pride.
My life shall live with beauty's light.
My life shall sport with reality's soul.
My life shall end with Divinity's height.

MY SKY AND MY SOUL

I have a sky, I have a sky.
Alas, no wings have I to fly.
Yet I have a sky, I have a sky.

I have a soul, I have a soul.
Alas, nowhere I see my Goal.
Yet I have a soul, I have a soul.

MY TASK

I ask my Lord Supreme, I ask:
What is my task, what is my task?
"My child, try and cry to change thy face,
And tell the world My Name is Grace."

Shall I succeed, can I succeed?
"Why not, why not? My Breath shall feed
Your life of love, devotion pure.
Victory all-where when surrender sure."

MARRIAGE

What is marriage?
  The smile of love
That allows two souls
  To soar above.

What is marriage?
  The curse of night.
A tug-of-war,
  No escape to Light.

What is marriage?
  God's fulfilment true.
In Silence and Power
  His Vision's due.

MY GOD IS STILL ALIVE

My God is still alive,
Again His Soul will thrive.
My God is still alive.

I've now the real medicine—
Surrendered love genuine.
I've now the real medicine.

Ever God and I will live.
I shall be and He will give.
Ever God and I will live.

ONE TRUTH

One truth to learn:
   Ignorance is naught.

One truth to follow:
   The path of Grace.

One truth to live:
   Forget Him not.

One truth to be:
   His Heart and Face.

OUR MEETING PLACE

O Lord, my Master-Love, how far are we,
How far from ecstasy's silence-embrace?
Heavy is my heart with sleepless sighs and pangs;
I know my bleeding core, our meeting place.

REVELATION

No more my heart shall sob or grieve.
My days and nights dissolve in God's own Light.
Above the toil of life, my soul
Is a bird of fire winging the Infinite.

I have known the One and His secret Play,
And passed beyond the sea of ignorance-dream.
In tune with Him, I sport and sing;
I own the golden Eye of the Supreme.

Drunk deep of Immortality,
I am the root and boughs of a teeming vast.
My Form I have known and realised.
The Supreme and I are one; all we outlast.

THE BOAT OF TIME SAILS ON

The sky calls me,
The wind calls me,
The moon and stars call me.

The green and dense groves call me,
The dance of the fountain calls me,
Smiles call me, tears call me,
A faint melody calls me.

The morn, noon and eve call me.
Everyone is searching for a playmate,
Everyone is calling me, "Come, come!"
One voice, one sound, all around.
Alas, the Boat of Time sails on.

THERE WAS A TIME

There was a time when I stumbled and stumbled,
But now I only climb and climb beyond
And far beyond my Goal's endless Beyond,
And yet my Captain commands: "Go on, go on!"

WHEN

When Peace once sang,
My world became my Father's Light.

When Love once sang,
My world became my Father's Delight.

When Truth once sang,
My world became my Father's Height.

WHERE

Where Peace once sang,
I became my Father's flowing Grace.

Where Love once sang,
I became my Father's glowing Face.

Where Truth once sang,
I became my Father's master Race.

WHERE IS THE TRUTH?

O Lord, where is the Truth?
"Where your Beloved is."
Who is my Beloved, who?
"In Whom your life is peace."

YOUR COMPASSION-WATERS

Peace, Peace,
Peace within my heart reigns supreme.
The soul-stirring flute of Lord Krishna
Is being played in my Heaven
And on my earth.

The destruction-shadows of dark demons
And the ignorance-delusion of sombre night
Lie long-buried in the depths
Of my body, mind, heart and life.
My aspiration-flames ever swim across
The expanse of Your Compassion-Waters.

MY GREEN-RED JOURNEY
AND
MY BLUE-GOLD JOURNEY

Before my green-red journey's
   Earth-bound flight,
My soul shook hands with God's
   Compassion-Height.

Before my blue-gold journey's
   Heaven-bound flight,
My life shakes hands with God's
   Perfection-Light.

I SING, I SMILE

I sing because You sing.
I smile because You smile.
Because You play on the flute,
I have become Your flute.
You play in the depths of my heart.
You are mine, I am Yours:
This is my sole identification.
In one Form
You are my Mother and Father eternal,
And Consciousness-moon, Consciousness-sun,
All-pervading.

I SHALL LISTEN

I shall listen to Your Command, I shall.
In Your Sky I shall fly, I shall fly.
Eternally You are mine, my very own.
You are my heart's wealth.
For You at night in tears I shall cry.
For You at dawn with light I shall smile.
For You, for You, Beloved, only for You.

MY DREAM WILL BE FULFILLED

My dream will be fulfilled
In the great festival
Of my surrender's consecration-fire.

Your Smile, Your Flute,
Your Banner, Your Consciousness-Light
In my world shall dance,
I know, I know.

O MY LORD OF BEAUTY

You are beautiful, more beautiful, most beautiful,
Beauty unparalleled in the Garden of Eden.
Day and night may Thy Image abide
In the very depth of my heart.
Without You my eyes have no vision—
Everything is an illusion, everything is barren.
All around me, within and without,
The melody of tenebrous pangs I hear.
My world is filled with excruciating pangs.
O Lord, O my beautiful Lord,
O my Lord of Beauty,
In this lifetime, even for a fleeting second,
May I be blessed with the boon
    To see Thy Face.

ONLY THE OTHER DAY

O Lord Supreme,
Only the other day
I saw You and played with You
Before I came into the world of ignorance-night.
Yet I remember my golden past
Within and without.
Alas, far, very far, now You are.
The bird of my heart is crying and trembling
With darkest pangs.

O MY BOATMAN

O my Boat, O my Boatman,
O message of Transcendental Delight,
  Carry me.
My heart is thirsty and hungry,
And it is fast asleep at the same time.
Carry my heart to the other shore.
The dance of death I see all around.
The thunder of destruction indomitable I hear.
O my Inner Pilot, You are mine,
You are the Ocean of Compassion infinite.
In You I lose myself,
My all in You I lose.

MY LAST WORD

My last word You will hear.
With this hope
I still exist on earth.
Let me dance in Your Heart always,
In the nights of sorrow and in the days of joy.
I feel that the torture of happiness is more painful
Than the torture of sorrow,
For when I am in joy I forget You;
I hurt Your Heart.

HOW LONG?

How long more shall I cry, Mother?
How long shall I cry
In a dark room alone, loving You?
You know my secret thoughts,
You know my heart's eagerness.
Why does dark death torture me every day?
How long will You delay, Mother?
How long will You delay?
As Jesus had Mary,
So are You my World-Mother.

YOUR NECTAR-COMPASSION

You are beautiful, O Being Absolute,
I am Your slave.
In Your Victory is my victory,
My endless rapture.
My heart has suffered infinite pangs to know You.
Therefore I hurl the arrows of my sulk-venom
　　At Your Heart.
Freed from errors, thought abolished,
No desire have I now.
O Beauty Transcendental,
I am the slave of Your Nectar-Compassion.

ONLY ONE HOPE

Break asunder all my hopes.
Only keep one hope,
And that hope is to learn
The language of Your inner Silence
In my utter, unconditional surrender.
In Your clear and free Sky
I shall be calm and perfect.
The bird of my heart is dancing today
In the festival of supernal Light.

GOD THEN

God then was Love,
  So nice and fine.
God then was mine,
  Below, above.

GOD NOW

God now is Light,
   Delight, Delight.
My All, my All,
   God now is Light.

I NEED YOU NOT

O Time and Space,
I need you not.
My breath has caught
My Supreme's Face.

O Depth and Height,
I need you not.
My soul has bought
Reality's Light.

O Golden Goal,
I need you not.
My Lord has sought
My Journey's Soul.

O IMAGINATION!

Imagination, O Imagination!
You are my life's adoration.
You I shall not keep afar.
Imagination, O Imagination!

In false, binding lies I shall not cry.
I shall not welcome
The life of impurity's ugliness.
With paltry victory
I shall not smile and rejoice.
Imagination, O Imagination!

To death's call I shall not respond.
The soul am I; no death have I.
No more, never,
Shall I walk along the wrong path.
Imagination, O Imagination!

FAITH AND DOUBT

O what is faith and what is doubt?
Faith is life-sun beyond the grave.
Doubt is the battle lost, within, without.
A doubter cries: "Me, none can save."

MOTHER, IF I LOSE TO YOU

Mother, if I lose to You,
That is my only victory.
Whatever I have given into Your Hands
Is my only savings.
To me the rest is of no value,
A mere waste,
And it only tortures me and
Stands as a burden on my way.
I cannot put it to use.
When I lose to You,
After I have achieved
My full realisation,
I know my greatest reward I shall receive.

FAREWELL TIME

It is farewell time;
The play of the heart will now begin.
The banner of divine Love
Will fly today in the boundless sky.
The sun, the moon, the deathless consciousness,
Infinity's secret wealth, the World-Lord's very Feet,
Far Heaven's blessing-message,
The flood of liberation,
The Abode of divine Nectar,
All will be united in the heart of our world.

THE PILGRIMS OF THE LORD SUPREME

We are the pilgrims of the Lord Supreme
   On the Path of Infinity.
At this time we have broken asunder
   Obstruction's door.
We have broken asunder the night
Of tenebrous darkness, inconscience
And the eternal, indomitable fear of death.
The Boat of the supernal Light's dawn
   Is beckoning us,
And the World-Pilot
Of the hallowed bond of Love divine
   Is beckoning us.
The Liberator's Hands are drawing us
   To the Ocean of the great Unknown.
Having conquered the life-breath
   Of the Land of Immortality,
And carrying aloft the Banner
   Of the Lord Supreme,
We shall return—
We, the drops and flames
   Of Transformation-Light.

MY FATHER-SON

O Supreme, my Father-Son,
Now that we two are one
And won by each other, won,
Nothing remains undone.

YOUR LOVE-PLAY IS MY WORLD

In secrecy supreme I see You.
You live in my eyes, in my sleep,
In my dreams, in my sweet wakefulness.
In the stupendous mirth of life,
In the abysmal lap of death,
You I behold.
Your Love-Play is my world.

ALTHOUGH

Although I teach, I am the cap of fools.
Although I love all souls, a fiend am I.
I am not strong, yet for the weak I fight.
At will I sell myself and myself I buy.

At every pause my life I contradict.
To me are ever the same all truths and lies.
To me the earthly beings and He are one.
We fly in His Bosom vast, in us He flies.

WHAT CAN I DO?

Heaven is afraid of me.
  What can I do?
I fly beyond its glee,
  Piercing the Blue.

Earth is afraid of me.
  What can I do?
I fell its ignorance-tree
  To plant the true.

Hell is afraid of me.
  What can I do?
My compassion frees its pangs
  From the racking screw.

My soul is afraid of me.
  What can I do?
Body's Eternity
  I know is due.

MY EGO AND MY SOUL

My ego needs,
My soul has.

My ego tries,
My soul does.

My ego knows the problem that is,
My soul becomes the answer that is.

I am not alone;
Within my unlit self,
My ego, my naked death.

I am not alone;
Within my snow-white heart,
My soul and my Spirit's flame.

I HAVE WORSHIPPED

I have worshipped God with love.
His Delight is my reward.

I have worshipped God with fear.
His sorrow is my result.

I have worshipped God to see Him.
He comes, but I see Him not.

I have worshipped God,
I know not why.
He is now won—
My self-revealing Sun.

PRECIOUS

Precious beyond measure is God's Will,
None can undo its Power.
Precious beyond measure are man's tears,
They alone can hug God's Hour.

Precious beyond measure is man's love,
Unveiling his golden face.
Precious beyond measure is God's Gift:
His all-fulfilling Grace.

TOMORROW'S STORY NOT THE SAME

In vain I seek, in vain I sought
To capture the flight of a fleeting thought.
In vain I seek, in vain I sought.

In vain I played, in vain I play
In the dun abyss of ignorance-clay.
In vain I played, in vain I play.

But tomorrow's story not the same:
My thoughts shall wed the Eternal Game.
But tomorrow's story not the same.

But tomorrow's story not the same.
Ignorance conquered, I shall tame.
But tomorrow's story not the same.

GOD AND THE WORLD

The world and God:
How to harmonise?
Difficult? No.
No wide surprise.

Our Father is God;
The world, our Mother.
This living truth
Our protecting cover.

Father is the Face;
Mother, the Smile.
Without the one,
The other futile.

I FEAR

I fear to speak, I fear to speak.
My tongue is killed, my heart is weak.

I fear to think, I fear to think.
My mind is wild and apt to sink.

I fear to see, I fear to see.
I eat the fruits of ignorance-tree.

I fear to love, I fear to love.
A train of doubts around, above.

I fear to be, I fear to be.
Long dead my life of faith in me.

MY GIANT PRIDE

In vain I try to sell my giant pride;
   No soul ventures to come forth.
My Beloved Lord, You try!
   This vital horse only You can ride.

The more my bosom aches, the more it grows.
   My hunger plays the fool.
My ignorance knows no school.
   The night of destruction piercing flows.

THOUGHT

Thought is the bridge
   Between Heaven and hell.
Thought is power,
   A ceaseless magic spell.

Thought is a tool
   To work out in human life.
Its gift is smile,
   Its triumph, wisdom's knife.

Action is the fruit
   Of thought sublime and poor
To open and close
   Our God's Compassion-Door.

LOVE IS THIS, ALSO LOVE IS THAT

Love is the road that leads
Our souls to union vast.
Love is the passion-storm
That sports with our vital dust.

Love's child is emotion-flame.
Love's eyes are freedom, fear.
Love's heart is breath or death.
And love is cheap, love dear.

I REMEMBER

I remember ...
My mother loved me, her world.
My father loved me, his dream.
My home loved me, its 'Supreme'.

I remember ...
I prayed with the blooming dawn,
I played with the glowing sun.
My life, the nectar-fun.

I remember ...
I sang with the twinkling stars,
I danced with the floating moon.
All lost, alas, too soon.

I remember, I remember, I remember.

THE GOLDEN FLUTE

A sea of Peace and Joy and Light
   Beyond my reach I know.
In me the storm-tossed weeping night
   Finds room to rage and flow.

I cry aloud, but all in vain;
   I helpless, the earth unkind!
What soul of might can share my pain?
   Death-dart alone I find.

A raft am I on the sea of Time,
   My oars are washed away.
How can I hope to reach the clime
   Of God's eternal Day?

But hark! I hear Thy golden Flute,
   Its notes bring the Summit down.
Now safe am I, O Absolute!
   Gone death, gone night's stark frown!

MASTER

O Lord of Nature, sovereign Sun of all!
　Who, if not Thou, will speak of Thee?
　Thy Smile of Grace through Eternity
Frees all aspiring souls from night's dumb call.

Reality unique! Thou art the ring
　Of the lowest chasm and spanless height.
　In Thee they feel their haven bright;
In Thee all beings move and wave and wing.

To see Thy all-transcending mystic Form,
　No vision have we of golden gaze;
　Thou art the Noon of all our days,
The veerless Pilot in our death's stark storm.

THE MESSAGE OF SURRENDER

Today You have given me
The message of surrender.
I have offered to You
My very flower-heart.
In the dark night with tears,
In the unknown prison-cell of illusion,
In the house of the finite,
No longer shall I abide.
I know You are mine.
I have known this, Mother,
O Queen of the Eternal.

INVOCATION

Supreme, Supreme, Supreme, Supreme!
  I bow to Thee, I bow.
  My life, Thy golden plough;
My journey's Goal, Thy soulful Dream.
Supreme, Supreme, Supreme, Supreme!
  I bow to Thee, I bow.

Supreme, I am Thy glowing Grace.
  My world, Thy Feet of Light;
  My breath, Thy Vision's kite.
Thou art one Truth, one Life, one Face.
Supreme, Supreme, Supreme, Supreme!
  I bow to Thee, I bow.

ALPHABETICAL INDEX OF TITLES

ABOUT THE AUTHOR

SRI CHINMOY is a fully realised spiritual Master dedicated to serving those seeking a deeper meaning in life. Through his teaching of meditation, his music, art and writings, his athletics and his own life of dedicated service to humanity, he tries to inspire others to find inner peace and fulfilment.

Born in Bengal in 1931, Sri Chinmoy entered an ashram (spiritual community) at the age of 12. His life of intense spiritual practice included meditating for up to 14 hours a day, together with writing poetry, essays and devotional songs, doing selfless service and practising athletics. While still in his early teens, he had many profound inner experiences and attained spiritual realisation. He remained in the ashram for 20 years, deepening and expanding his realisation, and in 1964 came to New York City to share his inner wealth with sincere seekers.

Today, Sri Chinmoy serves as a spiritual guide to disciples in more than 100 centres around the world. He advocates the path of the heart as the simplest way to make rapid spiritual progress. By meditating on the spiritual heart, he teaches, the seeker can discover his own inner treasures of peace, joy, light and love. The role of a spiritual Master, according to Sri Chinmoy, is to help the seeker live so that these inner riches can illumine his life. He instructs his disciples in the inner life and elevates their consciousness not only beyond their expectation, but even beyond their imagination. In return he asks his students to meditate regularly and to try to nurture the inner qualities he brings to the fore in them.

Sri Chinmoy teaches that love is the most direct way for a seeker to approach the Supreme. When a child feels love for his father, it does not matter how great the father is in the world's eye; through his love the child feels only his oneness with his father and his father's possessions. This same approach, applied to the Supreme, permits the seeker to feel that the Supreme and His Eternity, Infinity and Immortality are the seeker's own. This philosophy of love, Sri Chinmoy feels, expresses the deepest bond between man and God, who are aspects of the same unified consciousness. In the life-game, man fulfils himself in the Supreme by realising that God is his own highest self. The Supreme reveals Himself through man, who serves as His instrument for world transformation and perfection.

In the traditional Indian fashion, Sri Chinmoy does not charge a fee for his spiritual guidance, nor does he charge for his frequent concerts or public meditations. His only fee, he says, is the seeker's sincere inner cry. He takes a personal interest in each of his students, and when he accepts a disciple, he takes full responsibility for that seeker's inner progress. In New York, Sri Chinmoy meditates in person with his disciples several times a week and offers a regular weekly meditation session for the general public. Students living outside New York see Sri Chinmoy during worldwide gatherings that take place three times a year, during visits to New York, or during the Master's frequent trips to their cities. They find that the inner bond between Master and disciple transcends physical separation.

Sri Chinmoy accepts students at all levels of development, from beginners to advanced seekers, and lovingly guides them inwardly and outwardly according to their individual needs.

Sri Chinmoy personally leads an active life, demonstrating most vividly that spirituality is not an escape from the world, but a means of transforming it. He has written more than 1000 books, which include plays, poems, stories, essays, commentaries and answers to questions on spirituality. He has painted thousands of widely exhibited mystical paintings and composed more than 14,000 devotional songs. Performing his own compositions on a wide variety of instruments, he has offered a series of over five hundred Peace Concerts in cities around the world.

A naturally gifted athlete and a firm believer in the spiritual benefits of physical fitness, Sri Chinmoy encourages his disciples to participate in sports. Under his inspirational guidance, the international Sri Chinmoy Marathon Team organises hundreds of road races, including the longest certified race in the world (3,100 miles), and stages a biennial global relay run for peace.

For further information, please write to:
AUM PUBLICATIONS
86-10 Parsons Blvd.
Jamaica, NY 11432

GOD is...
Selected Writings of Sri Chinmoy

This long-awaited book gathers Sri Chinmoy's insights about God into one volume. These selections are drawn from the more than one thousand books he has written in over thirty years of teaching spirituality and meditation. His intimate knowledge of God transcends religious dogma and scripture, shedding light on all seekers' paths to God. The simplicity of the language embodies an astonishing depth of knowledge that goes beyond the intellect and directly communicates the wisdom of the soul.

Topics include: Can the existence of God be proven? • The cause of your separation from God • Should you ever fear God? • Seeing God in all • The meaning of suffering • Increasing your need for God • How to know what God wants you to do with your life. $12.95

The Three Branches of India's Life-Tree:
Commentaries on the Vedas, the Upanishads and the Bhagavad Gita

This book brings together in one volume Sri Chinmoy's commentaries on the Vedas, the Upanishads and the Bhagavad Gita, three ancient Indian scriptures which are the foundations of Hindu spiritual tradition. His approach is clear and practical, and at the same time profound and richly poetic. In a style unmistakably his own, Sri Chinmoy makes direct and personal contact with the reader, who joins him on a journey through the wisdom of these celebrated classics. This book is both an excellent introduction for readers who are coming to the subject for the first time, and a series of illumining meditations for those who already know it well. $13.95

Meditation: Man-Perfection in God-Satisfaction

Presented with the simplicity and clarity that have become the hallmark of Sri Chinmoy's writings, this book is easily one of the most comprehensive guides to meditation available.

Topics include: Proven meditation techniques that anyone can learn • How to still the restless mind • Developing the power of concentration • Carrying peace with you always • Awakening the heart centre to discover the power of your soul • The significance of prayer. Plus a special section in which Sri Chinmoy answers questions on a wide range of experiences often encountered in meditation. $9.95

Beyond Within:
A Philosophy for the Inner Life

"How can I carry on the responsibilities of life and still grow inwardly to find spiritual fulfilment?"

When your simple yearning to know the purpose of your life and feel the reality of God has you swimming against the tide, then the wisdom and guidance of a spiritual Master who has crossed these waters is priceless. Sri Chinmoy offers profound insight into man's relationship with God, and sound advice on how to integrate the highest spiritual aspirations into daily life.

Topics include: The transformation and perfection of the body • The spiritual journey • Meditation • The relationship between the mind and physical illness • Using the soul's will to conquer life's problems • How you can throw away guilt • Overcoming fear of failure • The purpose of pain and suffering • Becoming conscious of your own divine nature • The occult. $13.95

Death and Reincarnation

This deeply moving book has brought consolation and understanding to countless people faced with the loss of a loved one or fear of their own mortality. Sri Chinmoy explains the secrets of death, the afterlife and reincarnation. $7.95

Kundalini: The Mother-Power

En route to his own spiritual realisation, Sri Chinmoy attained mastery over the Kundalini and occult powers. In this book he explains techniques for awakening the Kundalini and the chakras. He warns of the dangers and pitfalls to be avoided and discusses some of the occult powers that come with the opening of the chakras.

$7.95

Yoga and the Spiritual Life

Specifically tailored for Western readers, this book offers rare insight into the philosophy of Yoga and Eastern mysticism. It offers novices as well as advanced seekers a deep understanding of the spiritual side of life. Of particular interest is the section on the soul and the inner life. $8.95

The Summits of God-Life: Samadhi and Siddhi

A genuine account of the world beyond time and space

This is Sri Chinmoy's firsthand account of states of consciousness that only a handful of Masters have ever experienced. Not a theoretical or philosophical book, but a vivid and detailed description of the farthest possibilities of human consciousness. Essential reading for all seekers longing to fulfil their own spiritual potential.

$6.95

Inner and Outer Peace
A powerful yet simple approach for establishing peace in your own life and the world

Sri Chinmoy speaks of the higher truths that energise the quest for world peace, giving contemporary expression to the relationship between our personal search for inner peace and the world's search for outer peace. He reveals truths which lift the peace of the world above purely political and historical considerations, contributing his spiritual understanding and inspiration to the cause of world peace. $7.95

Eastern Light for the Western Mind
Sri Chinmoy's University Talks

In the summer of 1970, in the midst of the social and political upheavals that were sweeping college campuses, Sri Chinmoy embarked on a university lecture tour offering the message of peace and hope embodied in Eastern philosophy. Speaking in a state of deep meditation, he filled the audience with a peace and serenity many had never before experienced. They found his words, as a faculty member later put it, "to be living seeds of spirituality." These moments are faithfully captured in this beautiful volume of 42 talks. $7.95

A Child's Heart and a Child's Dreams
Growing Up with Spiritual Wisdom—A Guide for Parents and Children

Sri Chinmoy offers practical advice on a subject that is not only an idealist's dream but every concerned parent's lifeline: fostering your child's spiritual life, watching him or her grow up with a love of God and a heart of self-giving.

Topics include: Ensuring your child's spiritual growth • Education and spirituality—their meeting ground • Answers to children's questions about God • A simple guide to meditation and a special section of children's stories guaranteed to delight and inspire. $7.95

The Master and the Disciple

What is a Guru? There are running gurus, diet gurus and even stock market gurus. But to those in search of spiritual enlightenment, the Guru is not merely an 'expert'; he is the way to their self-realisation. Sri Chinmoy says in this definitive book on the Guru-disciple relationship: "The most important thing a Guru does for his spiritual children is to make them aware of something vast and infinite within themselves, which is nothing other than God Himself."

Topics include: How to find a Guru • Telling a real spiritual Master from a false one • How to recognise your own Guru • Making the most spiritual progress while under the guidance of a spiritual Master • What it means when a Guru takes on your karma • Plus a special section of stories and plays illustrating the more subtle aspects of the subject. $7.95

Everest-Aspiration

These inspired talks by one who has reached the pinnacle are the best and surest guideposts for others who also want to go upward to the highest, forward to the farthest and inward to the inmost.

Topics include: Dream and Reality • Satisfaction • Imagination • Intuition • Realisation $8.95

Siddhartha Becomes the Buddha

Who exactly was the Buddha? In these ten dramatic scenes, Sri Chinmoy answers this question from the deepest spiritual point of view. The combination of profound insight and simplicity of language makes this book an excellent choice for anyone, young or old, seeking to understand one of the world's most influential spiritual figures. $5.95

Peace-Blossom-Fragrance
Aphorisms on Peace

These 700 aphorisms offer a profound and illumining look at the divine nature of peace, its relation to humanity's age-old quest, and secrets of its attainment and preservation. Special edition not available in stores.

          $7.95

My Lord's Secrets Revealed

This book consists of a series of brief, revealing glimpses of God the Supreme Father by a spiritual Master who has experienced them firsthand. Many of the revelations take the form of conversations between Sri Chinmoy, the son, and his all-loving Father. These conversations convey the loving intimacy between God and man. $7.95

Songs of the Soul

This volume brings together *Songs of the Soul* and *Blossoms of the Heart*. Each work has a lyric emphasis of its own, though the theme of both is our relationship with God. The poems in *Songs of the Soul* are luminous expressions from the innermost being, voicing its identity with the eternal Truth. Their appeal is a direct call to our own inner light. *Blossoms of the Heart* speaks to the upward-reaching aspiration in man, giving the seeker the assurance that his inner cry is never unheard.

$7.95

MUSIC OF SRI CHINMOY

Flute Music for Meditation

While in a state of deep meditation Sri Chinmoy plays his haunting melodies on the electric echo-flute. Its rich and soothing tones will transport you to the highest realms of inner peace and harmony.

Cassette $9.95   CD $12.95

Inner and Outer Peace

A tapestry of music, poetry and aphorisms on inner and outer peace. Sri Chinmoy's profoundly inspiring messages are woven into a calm and uplifting musical composition with the Master singing, chanting and playing the flute, harmonium, esraj, cello, harpsichord and synthesizer.

Cassette $9.95

Ecstasy's Trance
Esraj Music for Meditation

The esraj, often described as a soothing combination of sitar and violin, is Sri Chinmoy's favourite instrument. With haunting intensity, he seems to draw the music from another dimension. The source of these compositions is the silent realm of the deepest and most sublime meditation. Listen to the music and enter this realm, a threshold rarely crossed in the course of one's lifetime.

Cassette $9.95

The Dance of Light
Sri Chinmoy Plays the Flute
Forty-seven soft and gentle flute melodies that will carry
you directly to the source of joy and beauty: your own
aspiring heart. Be prepared to float deep, deep within on
waves of music that "come from Heaven itself."
                                                    Cassette $9.95

My Flute
Sri Chinmoy recites his poetry
In this remarkable collection of poetry, Sri Chinmoy
conveys the whole spectrum of spiritual emotions rang-
ing from the doubts and fears of the wavering pilgrim to
the ecstatic realisations of the illumined Master. In his
role as a Seer-Poet, Sri Chinmoy speaks with a power,
lyricism and authenticity seldom encountered in this
genre.   CD $9.95

To order books or tapes, request a catalogue, or find out
more about Sri Chinmoy or the Sri Chinmoy Centres
worldwide, please write to:

Aum Publications
86-10 Parsons Blvd.
Jamaica, NY 11432

When ordering a book or cassette, send check or money
order made out to Aum Publications. Please add $3.50
postage for the first item and 50¢ for each additional
item. Prices valid thru January 1999.